Contents

A rainforest habitat

A rainforest is an area of land.
A rainforest can be warm and wet.

A rainforest has living things.
A rainforest has non-living things.

Monkey

howler monkey

Is a monkey a living thing?

Does a monkey need food? *Yes.*
Does a monkey need water? *Yes.*

Does a monkey need air? *Yes.*

Does a monkey grow? *Yes.*

So a monkey is a living thing.

Stream

Is a stream a living thing?

Does a stream need food? *No*.
Does a stream need more water? *No*.

Does a stream need air? *No.*

Does a stream grow? *No.*

So a stream is not a living thing.

Tree

Is a tree a living thing?

Does a tree need food? *Yes*.
Does a tree need water? *Yes*.

Does a tree need air? *Yes.*

Does a tree grow? *Yes.*

So a tree is a living thing.

Butterfly

Is a butterfly a living thing?

nectar – butterfly food

Does a butterfly need food? *Yes.*
Does a butterfly need water? *Yes.*

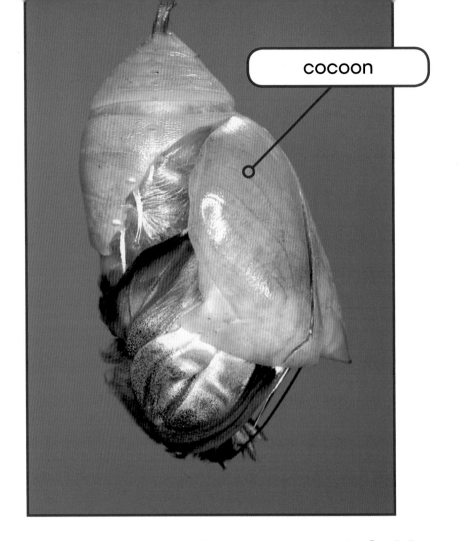

cocoon

Does a butterfly need air? *Yes.*

Does a butterfly grow? *Yes.*

So a butterfly is a living thing.

A rainforest is home to many things.
A rainforest is an important habitat.

Picture glossary

habitat area where plants and animals live

rainforest a habitat that can be warm and wet

stream small body of flowing water

Index

Notes for parents and teachers
Before reading
Talk to the children about rainforests. Have they seen them in books or on the TV? Talk about how lots of things grow in a rainforest because it is very warm and wet. Show the children a map or globe and point out the largest areas of rainforests.
After reading
Cut out pictures of things such as a cat, dog, tree, book, house, flower, and car. Ask the children to answer the key questions to determine if the thing is living or non-living (needs food, water, and air, and it grows). Help them to sort the pictures into two piles. Write "Living" and "Non-living" at the top of two sheets of paper. Ask the children to stick the pictures on the correct sheet.